The Developing

Artist

PIANO SONATINAS

BOOK THREE   Late Intermediate

A COMPREHENSIVE,
WELL-GRADED SERIES
OF AUTHENTIC
KEYBOARD SONATINAS.

Compiled and edited by

Nancy and Randall Faber

Production: Frank & Gail Hackinson
Production Coordinator: Marilyn Cole
Cover & Illustrations: Terpstra Design, San Francisco
Engraving: GrayBear Music Company, Hollywood, Florida
Printer: Vicks

PIANO ADVENTURES®

ISBN 978-1-61677-112-6

TABLE OF CONTENTS

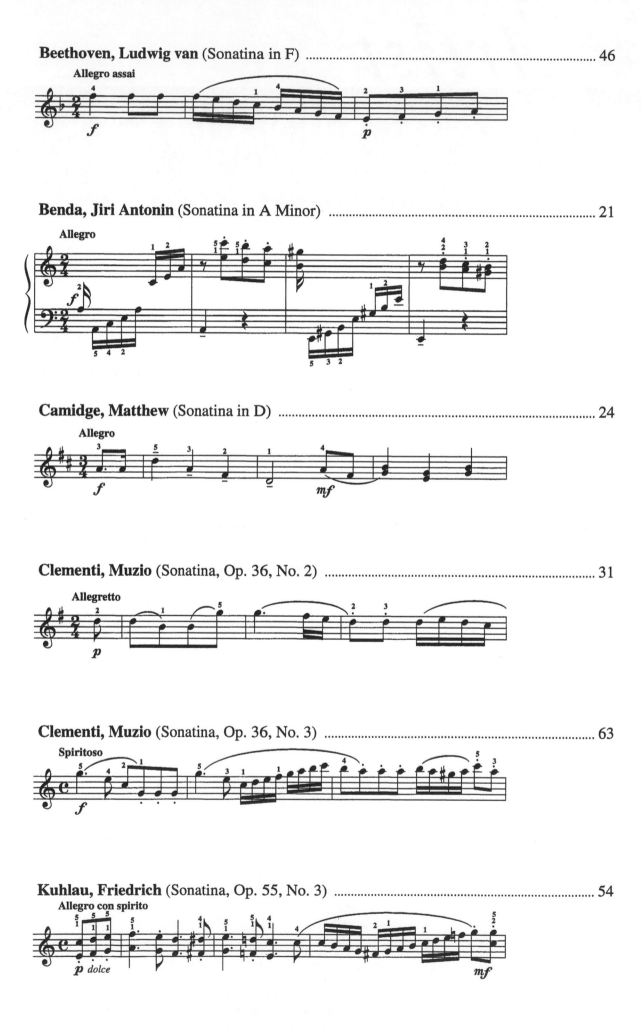

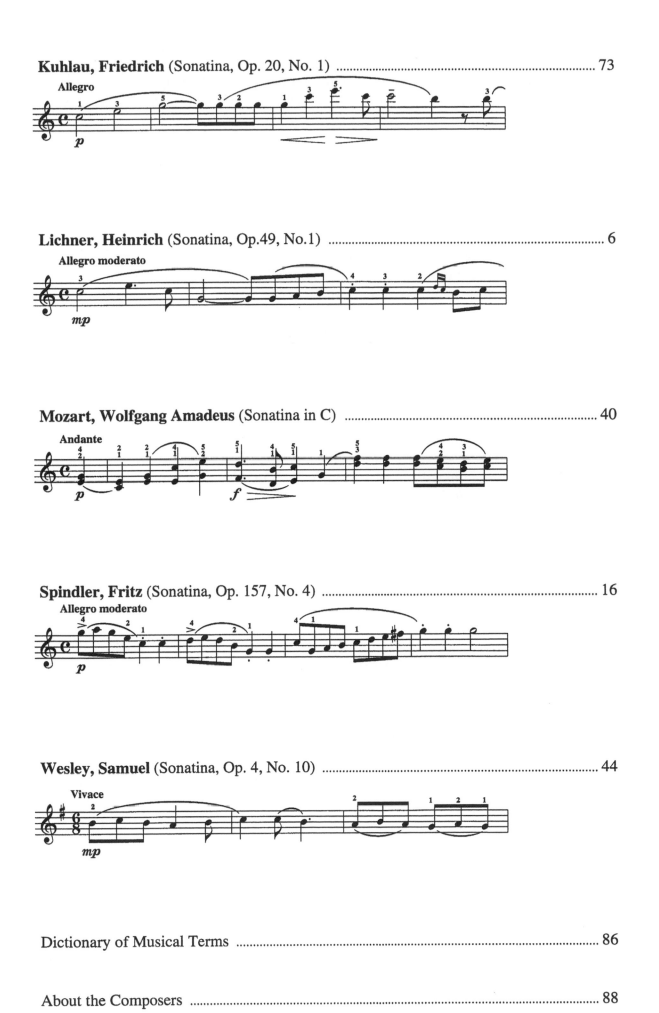

UNDERSTANDING MUSICAL FORM

Musical *form* is a way of organizing or structuring music. The following forms are common in classical sonatinas. You and your teacher may wish to refer to this page as you study the sonatinas in this book.

Binary (2-part) or AB form

The simplest musical form is one section of music followed by another section:
section A followed by **section B.** Each section usually has a repeat sign.
This 2-part (binary) form can be shown like this:

$$\| \mathbf{A} \| \mathbf{B} \|$$

Rounded binary form

This is still 2-part form, but with an interesting feature. In rounded binary form, the theme from section **A** returns *within* the **B** section.
It can be shown like this:

$$\| \mathbf{A} \| \mathbf{B} \ (A) \ \|$$ (**coda** optional)

Ternary form (3-part) or ABA form

Ternary means 3-parts: **section A, section B,** and the return of **section A.**
Ternary form is common in slow, lyric second movements.
This 3-part form can be shown like this:

$$\mathbf{A} \ \mathbf{B} \ \mathbf{A} \ (\mathbf{coda} \ \text{optional})$$

Rondo form

In this form, the A section reappears after each new section.
Rondo form is common for lively 3rd movements.
A typical rondo form looks like this:

$$\mathbf{A \ B \ A \ C \ A}$$

Sonata-allegro form

A more complex form, sonata-allegro form is used for first movements of sonatas and longer sonatinas. Many sonatinas, however, vary from precisely following the form.

In the first section, called the **exposition**, the themes are presented or "exposed." The 1st theme is usually followed with a more lyrical 2nd theme, usually in the key of the dominant. The exposition may end with a closing theme. The entire exposition is usually repeated.

The middle section is called the **development**. Themes or parts of themes may be presented in new keys or "developed" in imaginative ways. Shorter sonatinas may have only a transitional passage instead of a development section.

The final section is called the **recapitulation**. Here the themes are restated, or "recapped." Both the 1st and 2nd themes appear in the tonic key. Sometimes there are repeat signs at the end of the movement, which go back to the development. These are reminiscent of rounded binary form. It is common performance practice today, however, not to take this repeat.

A *coda* (ending) or *codetta* (short ending) will often end the movement.

Sonata-allegro form can be shown like this:

Exposition
> **1st theme**
> **2nd theme** (in the dominant)
> closing theme (in the dominant)

Development
> Themes are developed. Composers often use the following:
> key changes, frequent accidentals, parts of the theme (motifs),
> repetition, imitation, sequence

Recapitulation
> **1st theme** (in the tonic)
> **2nd theme** (in the tonic)
> closing theme (in the tonic)

Coda (optional)

Sonatina
Op. 49, No. 1

Heinrich Lichner
(1829-1898)

Exploring the Score: This movement is in *sonata-allegro* form. (See p.5.)

- With the help of your teacher, mark the following in your music:
  Exposition: 1st theme, 2nd theme (in the dominant), **closing theme**
  Development
  Recapitulation: 1st theme, 2nd theme (in the tonic), **closing theme**

II

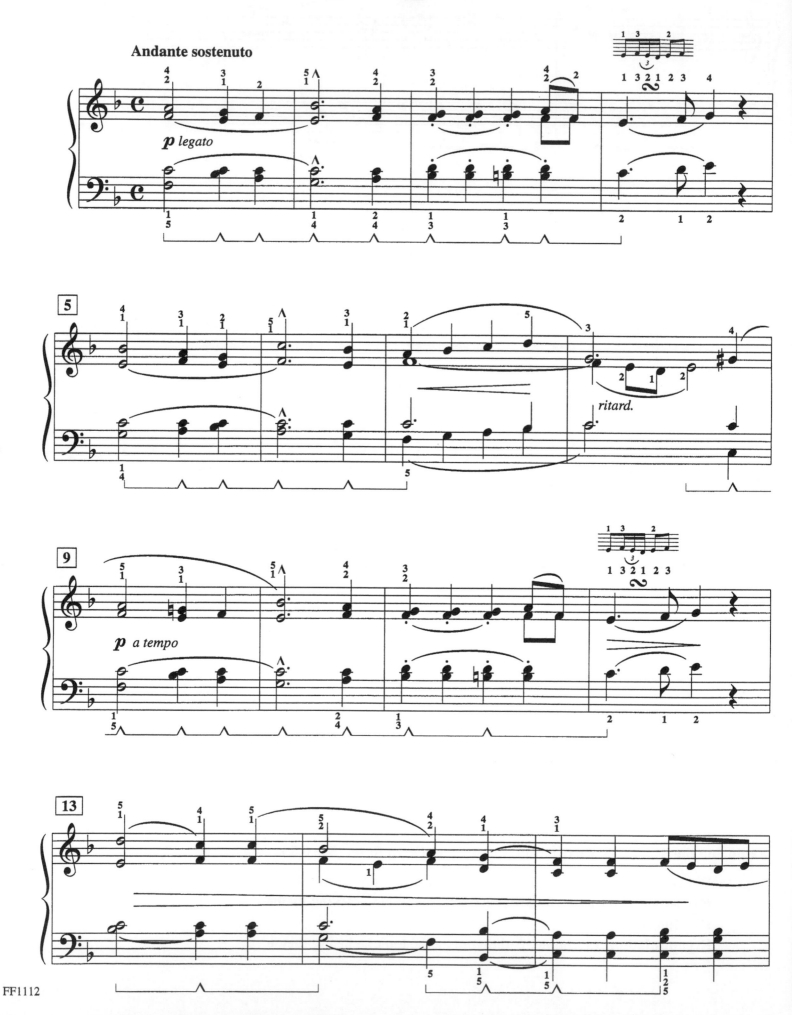

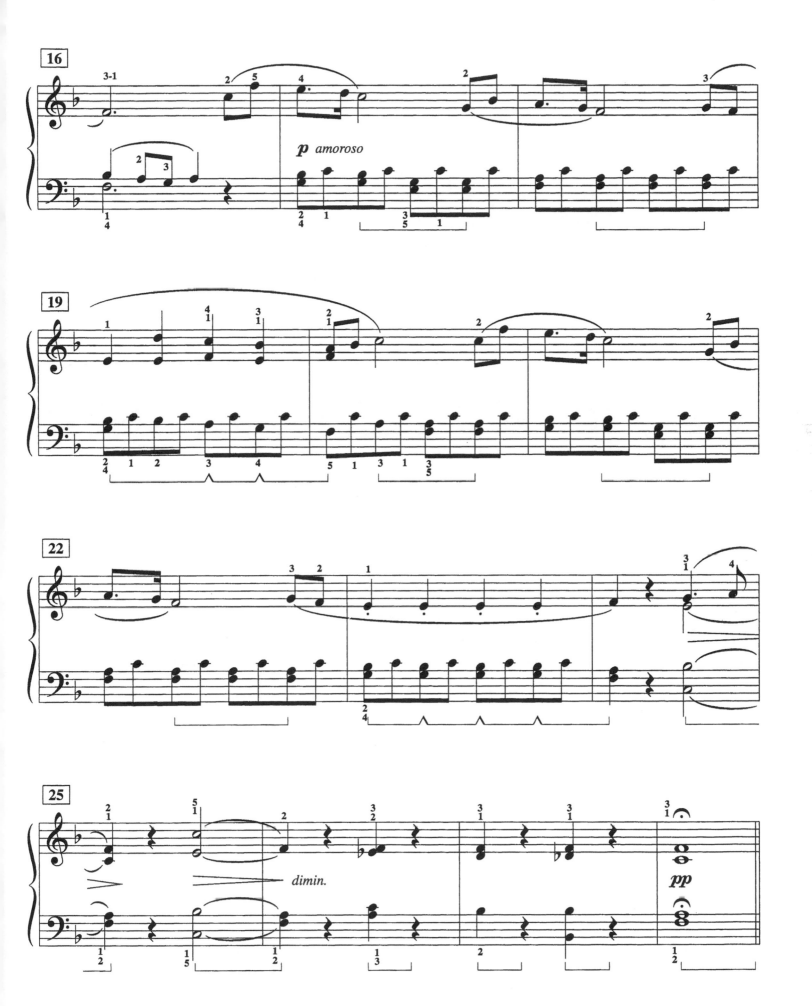

Exploring the Score: The form of this piece is **A B** with a *codetta* (a short *coda*).

- Mark these sections in your music.

III

Rondo

14

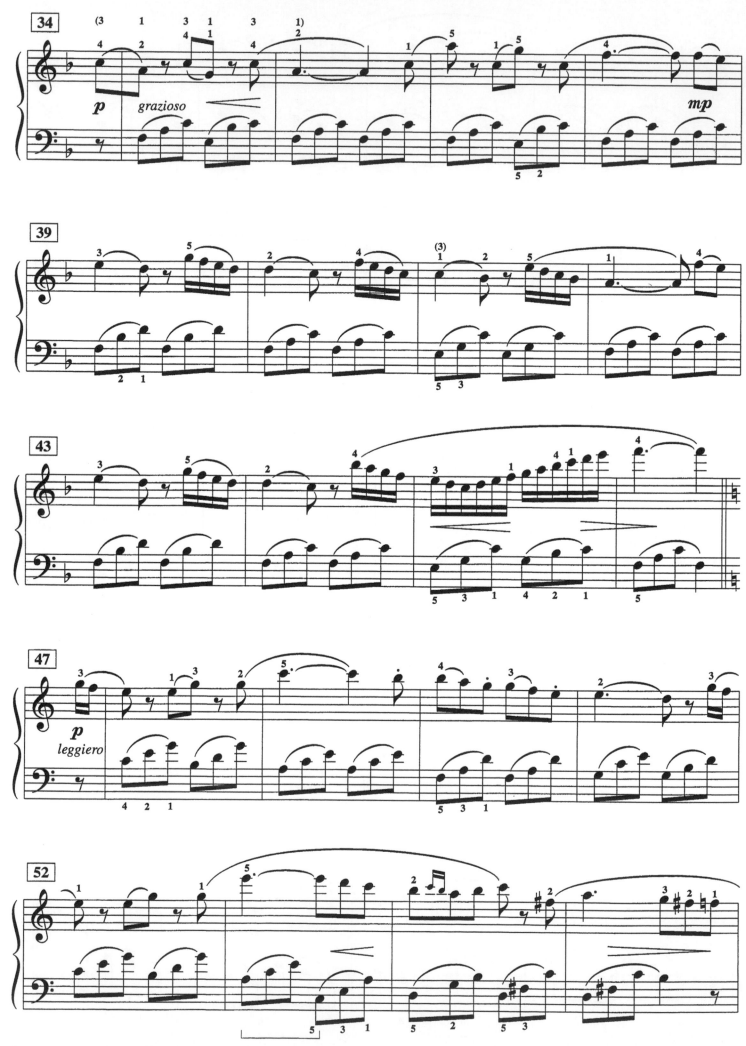

Exploring the Score: This movement is in rondo form: **A B A C A coda**

- Mark each section in your music.

- The scale passages in the *coda* are related to which section of the rondo? ____

Sonatina
Op. 157, No. 4

Fritz Spindler
(1817-1905)

Exploring the Score: The B section of this sonatina "develops" the opening *motif* (short musical idea) in a clever way. The motif is inverted (turned upside-down).

- Show your teacher how this motif is used in *imitation* between the hands.

- Can you find at least two *sequences* played by the right hand?

II

Exploring the Score: Circle the form of this rondo:

ABACA   ABACA coda   ABACABA

Sonatina in A Minor

Jiri Antonin Benda
(1722-1795)

Exploring the Score: Where does the opening theme appear in the key of C major? *measure* ___

Sonatina in D

Matthew Camidge
(1764-1844)

* The eighth notes are not necessarily intended as 2 against 3, but may be played as ♩♪.

Exploring the Score: This movement is in *sonata-allegro* form.

- Mark the following in your music:

    Exposition: 1st theme, 2nd theme (in the dominant), **closing theme**

    Development

    Recapitulation: 1st theme, 2nd theme (in the tonic), **closing theme**

II

La Chasse

Exploring the Score: This form of this piece is somewhat unusual: **A B C A coda.**

- Find and mark each section in your music.

Sonatina
Op. 36, No. 2

Muzio Clementi
(1752-1832)

Exploring the Score: This movement is in *sonata-allegro* form.

- Mark the following in your music:
  Exposition: 1st theme, 2nd theme (in the dominant)
  Development
  Recapitulation: 1st theme, 2nd theme (in the tonic)

II

Exploring the Score: Point out the **A section, B section,** and **return of the A section.**

III

Exploring the Score: Where does this piece move to the key of the dominant (D major)?

Hint: Look for the leading tone, C♯.

Sonatina in C

Wolfgang Amadeus Mozart
(1756-1791)

Exploring the Score: Circle the correct form of this piece:

Binary with coda   **Rounded binary** with coda   **A B A** with coda

II

Rondo

Exploring the Score: Mozart harmonized this rondo using only:

       I, IV and **V** chords   or   **I** and **V** (or **V7**) chords   (circle one)

Sonatina
Op. 4, No. 10

Pastorale

Samuel Wesley
(1766-1837)

Exploring the Score: Point out the **A B A** form of this piece.

Does the lengthy B section develop the A theme?

Sonatina in F

Ludwig van Beethoven
(1770-1827)

Exploring the Score: In the recapitulation, one of the themes does not reappear.

- Which theme is missing? **1st theme** or **2nd theme** (circle one)

II

Rondo

Exploring the Score: Label the sections of this rondo in your music. (**A B A C A codetta**)

Extra Credit: In section C, Beethoven uses another form you have learned. Circle the correct answer:

Binary   **Rounded binary**   **Ternary**

Sonatina
Op. 55, No. 3

Friedrich Kuhlau
(1786-1832)

Exploring the Score: The development draws mainly from which theme of the exposition?

1st theme   **2nd theme**   (circle one)

II

Allegretto grazioso

Exploring the Score: Study this rondo carefully and label each of the following sections in your music:

A   B   A   C   A   B   A

(development)

Sonatina
Op. 36, No. 3

Muzio Clementi
(1752-1832)

Exploring the Score: Label the sections of sonata-allegro form in your music.

Exposition: 1st theme, 2nd theme (in the dominant), **closing theme**

Development

Recapitulation: 1st theme, 2nd theme (in the tonic), **closing theme**

Extra Credit: How is the first measure of the development related to the 1st theme?

II

Exploring the Score: Name the form of this piece. _____

III

Exploring the Score: Label the 1st and 2nd themes. Point out the rhythmic similarity of the first
two measures in each theme.

Sonatina
Op. 20, No. 1

Freidrich Kuhlau
(1752-1832)

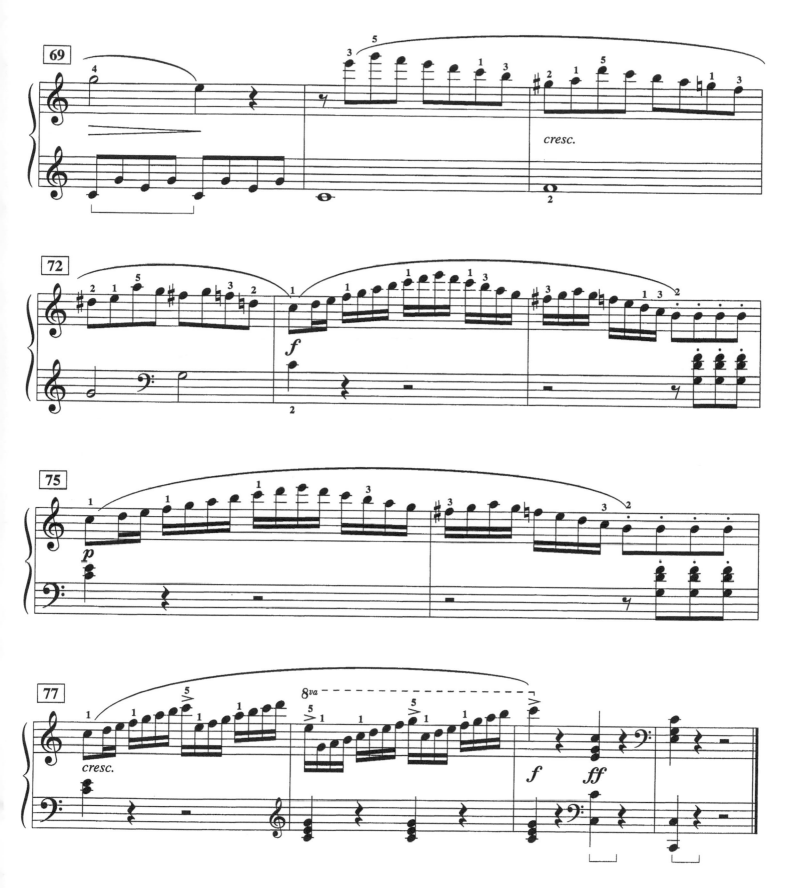

Exploring the Score: Mark the sonata-allegro form sections in your music.

Exposition: 1st theme, 2nd theme (in the dominant), **closing theme**

Development

Recapitulation: 1st theme, 2nd theme (in the tonic), **closing theme**

II

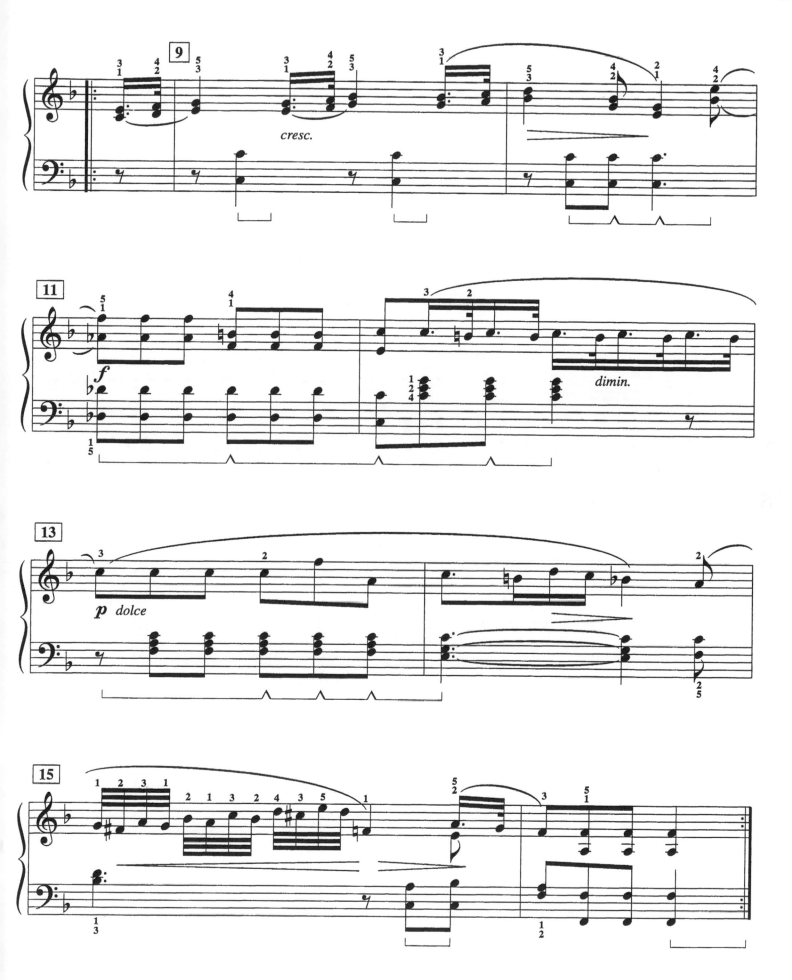

Exploring the Score: Circle the correct form:

        Binary   **Rounded binary**   **Ternary**

III

Rondo

Exploring the Score: Label the sections of this 7-part rondo plus coda in your music.

A   B   A   C   A   B   A   coda

Extra Credit: The material of the coda is related to which rondo section? _____

DICTIONARY OF MUSICAL TERMS

Adagio	*Andante*	*Moderato*	*Allegretto*	*Allegro*	*Vivace*
slowly	walking tempo	moderate tempo	rather fast	fast	very fast

SIGN	TERM	DEFINITION
accel.	*accelerando*	Gradually play faster.
>	**accent**	Play this note louder.
^	**sharp accent**	Play detached, with a strong accent.
	Alberti bass	A left hand accompaniment which outlines the notes of a chord using the pattern: bottom-top-middle-top. The *Alberti bass* was popularized during the Classic period.
₵	*alla breve*	Cut time. Short for ₂/₂ time signature. The half note gets the beat. (Two half note beats per measure.)
	allegro moderato	Moderately fast.
	amoroso	Tenderly.
	appoggiatura	An ornament which looks like a grace note without a slash, but is played on the beat and shares the duration of the principal note. An appoggiatura resolves a dissonance to a consonance.
	assai	Much. For example, *allegro assai* means "quite fast."
	a tempo	Return to the beginning tempo (speed).
	binary form	A musical form with 2 sections. (See page 4.)
	cadenza	An elaborate, showy passage played with rhythmic freedom.
	coda	Ending section. (A short *coda* is called a *codetta*.)
———	*crescendo (cresc.)*	Get gradually louder.
	con spirito	With spirit.
———	*decrescendo*	Get softer. Same as *diminuendo*.
———	*diminuendo. (dim. or dimin.)*	Get gradually softer.
	dolce	Sweetly.
	dominant	Step 5 of the scale (indicated with the Roman numeral V).
⌢	*fermata*	Hold this note longer than usual.
fz	*forzando*	Forced, accented.
	grace note	A decorative note, written in small type with a slash through the stem. Grace notes are played quickly, usually before the main tone. (See also *appoggiatura*.)
	grazioso	Gracefully.
	imitation	The restatement of a musical idea in a different "voice" (different hand or instrumental part).

SIGN	TERM	DEFINITION
	legato	Smoothly, connected.
	leggiero	Light and nimble.
	motif	Short musical idea.
Op.	**opus**	Work. A composer's compositions are often arranged in sequence, with each work given an opus number. Several pieces may be included in a single opus. Example: Op.3, No.1; Op.3, No.2, etc.
	pastorale	A piece imitating the music of shepherds, usually in $\frac{6}{8}$ time.
	phrase	A musical idea. Think of a phrase as a "musical sentence." It is shown in the music with a slur, also called a phrase mark.
	poco	A little.
	poco a poco	Little by little.
rall.	**rallantando**	Gradually slow down. Same as *ritardando*.
rit.	**ritardando (ritard.)**	Gradually slow down.
	rondo	The form for a piece that has a recurring A Section. Ex: ABACA
	rounded binary form	See page 4.
	sequence	A short musical pattern that is repeated on another pitch.
sfz or *sf*	*sforzando*	A sudden strong accent.
	slur	Connect the notes over or under a slur.
	sonata	An instrumental piece, usually with 3 movements.
	sonata-allegro form	A musical form commonly used for first movements. See page 5.
	sonatina	A little sonata.
	staccato	Play *staccato* notes detached; disconnected.
	staccato	The wedge was used by some early composers as a staccato mark. Same meaning as above.
sub.	*subito*	Suddenly.
	tempo	The speed of the music.
ten.	*tenuto*	Hold the note its full value.
	tenuto mark	Hold this note its full value. Press gently into the key.
∽	**turn**	A musical ornament that "turns" above and below the given note.
tr	**trill**	A quick repetition of the principal note with the note above it. (The number and speed of the repetitions depends on the music.)
	vivo	Fast and lively.

About The Composers

Ludwig van Beethoven (1770-1827)

Beethoven is one of the most well-known composers in history. He was born in Germany and studied with Haydn in Vienna. In spite of severe hearing loss which began in his mid 20's, Beethoven was a prolific composer. He even composed when totally deaf, though the condition shortened his career as a performer and conductor. His works include: 9 symphonies, 32 piano sonatas, 5 piano concertos, numerous chamber works, instrumental works, a ballet, an opera, other choral works, and 16 string quartets.

Jiri Antonin Benda (1722-1795)

Benda was a well-known Czech composer. His music often had dramatic, contrasting sections.

Matthew Camidge (1764-1844)

Camidge was an English organist and composer. He wrote many teaching pieces and a keyboard method.

Muzio Clementi (1752-1832)

Clementi was a highly successful pianist and composer. He was born in Rome, educated in England, and toured widely throughout Europe. He established a publishing company and piano factory in England, and achieved lasting fame with his compositions and exercises for piano students.

Friedrich Kuhlau (1786-1832)

Kuhlau was born in Germany and spent most of his life as a court musician in Copenhagen. He wrote many piano pieces and compositions for flute.

Heinrich Lichner (1829-1898)

Lichner is known for the many teaching pieces he composed. He was a German pianist, composer, and teacher.

Wolfgang Amadeus Mozart (1756-1791)

Mozart was a child prodigy who made his first public appearances at age 6 and had his first composition published at age 7. Wolfgang studied keyboard and violin with his father Leopold Mozart, also a composer. Though he died at the early age of 35, Wolfgang Amadeus Mozart left a legacy of nearly 50 symphonies, a dozen operas, 25 piano concertos, 42 violin sonatas, 23 string quartets, 17 piano sonatas, and many more musical works.

Fritz Spindler (1817-1905)

Spindler was a German pianist, composer, and very successful teacher. He is remembered for the piano pieces he wrote for his students.

Samuel Wesley (1766-1837)

A child prodigy, Wesley was considered by some to be an English Mozart. Samuel's uncle was the famous John Wesley, founder of the Methodist church. Samuel began music lessons at age six and became a prolific composer for the organ, harpsichord, and chorus.